I0004640

Windows 10

The Ultimate Crash Course to Learning Microsoft's Intelligent New Operating System

(Windows guide, Tips and tricks, Windows for beginners)

by James Clark

Table of Contents

Disclaimer

While all attempts have been made to verify the information provided in this book, the author does not assume any responsibility for errors, omissions, or contrary interpretations of the subject matter contained within. The information provided in this book is for educational and entertainment purposes only. The reader is responsible for his or her own actions and the author does not accept any responsibilities for any liabilities or damages, real or perceived, resulting from the use of this information.

Introduction

Windows. Along with its parent company Microsoft, Windows has been a household name for well over twenty years. During that time, it has had many ups and downs, going from being the gold standard of user friendly operating systems (OS), to universally derided bloatware and back again.

Windows 10, released in 2015 aims to bring the venerable OS back once more to glory. This is no small task given the less than positive response to the mobile friendly Window 8. The reception of Windows 8 was so poor that the folks at Redmond decided to skip right over Windows 9 in an effort to demonstrate a clean break with its predecessor.

Did they succeed? In a nutshell, yes. In this guide, we will be going over some of the changes Microsoft made that make Windows 10, while more of an organic development than a revolution, a worthwhile upgrade. We'll also be spending some time with brand new features like Microsoft Edge, Groove Music and more.

Finally, we'll let you in on some tips and tricks that will help you get the absolute most out of your new operating system and give you a peak what is coming in the soon to be (or recently released depending on when you are reading this) Anniversary Update.

Now, find your favorite computer chair and roll up to your desk or curl up with your laptop (or Surface) as we pull back the curtain on Windows 10.

Chapter 1 – Apps and Overview

There are a lot of new apps in Windows 10 that new users will be familiar with. Also, if you are upgrading straight from Windows 7, the mobile format will take some getting used to. Here, we'll walk you through some of those apps and talk about the overall look of the interface.

Getting Started

If you need a head start on figuring out what is new in your new OS, you can open up the Getting Started app that offers walkthroughs of many aspects of the operating system. If we miss anything that you are interested in, check it out for a quick look at whatever app you are wanting to get more information on.

The Look

One of the biggest complaints of Windows 8 was the default "tile" setting. Rather than a traditional desktop with a number of icons grouped along the left side of the screen, the whole screen was full of often oversized tiles optimized for touchscreens.

This was jarring for the average user who did not, and likely did not want to own a Windows mobile device. Finding this tablet-friendly design upon booting up a brand new desktop computer did not leave many people happy.

The truth is, there was a way to switch to a desktop mode but it was difficult to find.

Microsoft heard these complaints and designed their latest OS to sense what sort of environment it was operating in. So if you are running a Surface Pro 3, it knows that it is on a mobile device and presents the tile format by default.

If you are running a desktop computer, it will know that as well and boot up in a traditional desktop format. I run both a Surface Pro 3 and a desktop (sporting a 1st gen Intel i7) so I have seen this work first hand.

Should you desire to switch formats (as I sometimes do depending on what I'm doing), Microsoft has made this easy. Simply swipe your finger or mouse from the right side of the screen and it will bring up a number of Quick Actions, among them being the option to switch from tablet to desktop mode. One click and the format changes.

It also simple to customize the tiles. A right click or holding your finger on a given tile will bring up a menu that allows to you to remove it from the screen or resize it as desired. You can also move the tile around the screen and group them together however you like. Adding and removing them is simple as well and very intuitive.

Another feature is that many apps utilize live tiles. This means that certain apps, such as a news aggregator will constantly display images and headlines of stories based on your selected interests. Other apps that make use of this are Sports, Money, Weather, Netflix and Outlook. And don't worry. If you find that the tiles constantly flipping is distracting you from actually getting anything done, you can turn them off.

The Triumphant Return of the Start Menu

Remember that nice little menu with all of your programs (remember referring to software as "programs" instead of "apps?") stacked up in alphabetical order? Just click the little

Windows icon in the bottom left and there it was? Remember how great that was?

If so, then you might have heard that for reasons that no mere mortal truly knows, Microsoft got rid of it in Windows 8. Something about mobile is the future, tiles, blah, blah, blah. Fortunately, they heeded the cries of users the world over and put the Start Menu back in all of its glory.

In tablet mode, you find it by clicking on the list icon in the bottom left and you can then choose between letting it display only the most frequently used apps or all of them. Desktop does that and also gives you your tiles to the right of the list. And yes, you can customize them the same there as when in tablet mode.

This is definitely a much simpler way of navigating all the apps without having to either enter the app into the search bar, or pin a tile for every app to the start screen, eventually leading to having to scroll through several screens worth of tiles in order to find the one you are looking for.

And if you need for room for tiles so can easily access even more, just bring your mouse to the edge of the menu and drag it up or to the side to make it as large our small as you wish.

The Media is the Message

Windows 10 also comes with some decent media apps, Groove Music and the unimaginatively titled Movies & TV.

Like many music apps, Groove will search your hard drive for any music and automatically add it to its library. This includes music purchased through Groove, Amazon or uploaded from your own collection. There is also a monthly music subscription so that you never run out of tunes to listen to.

You can also add this music to your OneDrive account which will allow you to play it from any networked device that you have the OneDrive app installed on. And that can be almost any networked device as you can find a OneDrive app in the Google Play Store and Apple App Store.

Adding files to your OneDrive isn't quite as simple as it should be (at least not on my Surface) but it does work.

Movies & TV works similarly, aggregating anything you already have one your drive, including exports from video editing software.

Both apps have links to the appropriate area of the Microsoft Store so that you can readily purchase and download new music, movies and TV whenever it works with your schedule, wherever you are.

You can also access the Store via its own app within Windows 10. This is extremely handy in that if you find yourself in need of a photo editor, or a quick game to play, they are both only a click away.

Purchasing within the Microsoft Store has certain advantages. One is that all apps in the store have passed Microsoft's security requirements. Another is that you only need to purchase the program once and you can use it on any Windows device the app is designed for.

It is true that the Store is limited in its selection, as many have pointed out. This is only a real problem for a little while though, especially for laptop and tablet users. When it comes to such devices, it is important to recall that while they may be mobile devices, they are also both running the full version of Windows and as such are really able to download any Windows program available, whether it is in the Store or not. This fact is one of those that drew me back into Windows after about a decade of using any other OS besides the one from Redmond.

Internet Explorer is Dead. Long Live Microsoft Edge.

Another of the biggest changes in Windows 10 is the death of Internet Explorer and the introduction of Edge as its replacement. Much like skipping from 8 to 10, this is something of a symbolic move, signaling a break with the old and the introduction of something far better.

In truth it is really more of a few steps forward to catch up to features that long time users of Chrome and Firefox will already be familiar with. Still, it is an improvement and some features bear mentioning here.

Tabs – Rather than having a new window open for every single site you are visiting, you can simply open a new tab, a feature that definitely keeps the screen clean and other open apps easier to find.

Frequent sites – When you open a new tab, a row of frequently visited sites will also appear near the top of the screen. If you are just hoping online to check a few things, this is a big time saver.

News – The default homepage is MSN news. While any given headline or article may not be your cup of tea, it is handy if you want a quick look at what is going on out in the world.

Search – Just as with Chrome, you can now type a search straight into the address bar, rather than having to go to Bing or Google's search page first. Another significant time saver if you are going to be searching for multiple items or topics. Naturally, since this is Microsoft, the default search uses Bing rather than Google. Also, I have found that this feature works better on my desktop than it does on my Surface.

Reading view – Up by the address bar, you will find a little icon that looks suspiciously like an open book. If you click on it, the webpage that you are on will be converted to a text and picture format free of ads and those blasted pop-up videos.

I personally think this is a great feature as some of the sites I visit will frequently have a number of videos that will play with no input from myself, often while already watching another video on the same page.

Write on the Web - By clicking on the writing mode icon, you can use your mouse, finger, or Surface Pen (the last two assuming you have a touchscreen of course) to circle, underline, highlight, and add notes to any webpage, the same as you would with any book. You can then save your notes for later reference.

Cortana

Cortana is Microsoft's Siri. Or rather, Siri is Apple's Cortana since Microsoft actually beat Apple to the punch by about a year. However, since almost no one owns a Windows phone, almost no one knew anything about Cortana.

Just as with Siri, you can ask Cortana to search the internet for specific information, have it set notifications for you and open up various apps.

Also like Siri, you will need to spend some time training the software to understand your voice. Fair warning here, unless you have a microphone that is intended to work with the software, results will be spotty at best.

Unfortunately, my Surface Pro 3 does not fall into that category so I can't say I have used it very much, though recent updates seem to have improved its functionality. If the voice recognition does turn out to be more trouble than it is worth, you can always type in commands.

If you allow Cortana to know your location, it will give you weather info, news and movie reviews. It will also pay attention to what you pay attention to, further customizing its content the more you use the feature.

The Getting Started app has many videos outlining numerous different ways to use your new digital assistant.

OneDrive

You might remember OneDrive from the section on media apps. Much like Dropbox, or iCloud, you can use OneDrive to upload your images, documents, videos or anything else to the cloud so that you can access the files latter on from any device that has the OneDrive app. Adding files for the most part is only a drag and drop action, making it as painless as possible.

Reading List

This app allows you to save pages from Flipboard, Edge or any other compatible app, allowing you to pause reading that article on the Kardashians so that you can focus on something more important and go back what's going on with Khloe once the important work is done.

XBOX

You may have noticed that game consoles have been getting more and more like PCs for a while now. They have hard drives, RAM and the ability to surf the web. Now, you can even play your XBOX games on your Windows 10 PC. The app even lets you sync achievements, friend lists and all the things you expect in the age of multiplayer.

Through the Game Bar (access using Windows + G), the XBOX app also lets you record the activity on your screen. You can also make use of the Game Bar as another way to get screen shots.

Hello There

Windows Hello lets you use your fingerprint, iris, or face to login to your computer. Naturally, you will need the appropriate peripherals to support this feature. Unless of course you plan on getting a Surface Pro 4 or Surface Book, which come already equipped with a fingerprint reader.

Action Center

This is a handy area where many notifications will be displayed. Again, these can be configured to your preferences, allowing you to quickly check for new mail, news items, flight reminders, software updates and of course the weather.

Below the notification section is a number of tiles allowing quick access to various settings. The Wi-Fi tile is especially useful for those on-the go from one Wi-Fi hotspot to another.

Chapter 2 – Tips and Tricks

Anyone who knows even the slightest bit about computers knows that there are always a few dozen shortcuts and mini-features present in any program, things that most of us would never stumble across.

We find one way to get something done (probably the same way we've been doing it since our first computer) and keep chugging along, all the while unaware that there may be a better way of doing things hiding right under our noses. Let's take a look at a few of them.

Multi-tasking

Snap Assist – This is a feature I use almost every time I login to my Surface. Simply use your finger to drag an app over to the side of the screen and it will fit itself to half the screen. Any open apps will then be displayed in Task View on the second half of the screen, allowing you to select which one you would like to be filling up the other half.

This works a little different in desktop mode. In desktop mode, you can drag the app with your finger or mouse to a corner, at which point it adjusts to a quarter screen, allowing you to have four apps up and running and easy to access without a lot of cumbersome resizing with the mouse.

Both modes are useful if you are needing to do two things at once, such as researching a topic for a book you are in the process of writing.

Task view – There is an icon down in your task bar that looks a bit like a tri-fold display. Clicking on that will display all of your open apps in a thumbnail format, allowing you to quickly find the app you are looking for.

Background scrolling – This lets you scroll through any open app, whether it is in the foreground or not. No, this does not mean that you can scroll through apps in Task View. Maybe in an upcoming update.

Alt + Tab – For those who prefer to keep their hands on the keyboard, this shortcut does much the same thing as Task View. The big difference is that if you keep holding the Alt button while tapping Tab, each app will be highlighted, allowing you to find and bring up any open app extremely quickly.

This feature has actually been around for a long time but it is so little known that it is worth mentioning here. I've been using it myself lately and find it the most efficient way to sort through my open apps.

Virtual desktops – Do you have trouble staying away from Skype or your favorite casual game when you really should be working? Well, you can minimize that by making use of this little feature in desktop mode.

Hitting the task icon and then the big + in the bottom right corner of the screen will let you choose between and set up brand new desktops. That way you can keep business and pleasure separated on the same computer.

Keyboard Shortcuts

In addition to the beauty of Alt + Tab, there are a number of other shortcuts in Windows 10, most of them centering on the use of the Windows key. As with other features discussed in this guide, some work in both tablet and desktop modes, while others only function well in desktop mode.

Windows + X – Brings up a list of features like Task Manager, Computer Management, Disk Management, Command Prompt and more. This menu is also accessible by right clicking the start button.

Windows + C – Launches Cortana's voice recognition.

Windows + D – Clears the screen and shows the desktop (desktop mode only).

Windows + I – Brings up the standard setting menu. Not god mode, just the normal settings.

Windows + S – Brings up the search bar and Cortana's home page. Windows + Q does the same thing.

Windows + E – Launches File Explorer.

Windows + P – This bring up a menu on the right that lets you decide how to best utilize an extra/external monitor.

Windows + H – Allows you to take and share a screenshot of your work. This is much less cumbersome than using the snipping tool.

Windows + L – Locks the screen.

Windows + Arrow keys – Doing this in desktop mode lets you move your apps around the same as the Snap Assist described above.

Windows – Just tapping this button in tablet mode lets you alternate between the desktop (or home screen if you prefer) and whatever you had on the screen before that.

There are other commands that are worth learning. The best thing that you can do is simply play around with the Windows, Ctrl, and Alt keys to find out what little nuggets Microsoft has hidden in there.

If you take the time to learn and practice them, they will definitely increase your productivity and decrease your frustration levels as you will not spend as much time going from the keyboard to the mouse and more importantly, not have to hunt through hordes of menus to find the features you are looking for.

Behold the Power of God Mode

Yes, Windows 10 has a god mode. No, you will not instantly be able to create new realities *ex nihilo* (not even digital ones) it is useful if you are trying to make adjustments to your system and are having a really hard time finding the setting you are looking for.

This is actually a common complaint with Windows in its last few iterations. Whereas at one time all you had to do was open the Control Panel and you could find any setting you wanted, recent changes have made the menus easier to navigate for casual users, resulting in many setting getting buried.

This isn't a huge problem for power users who always seem to be able find what they need. However, for those of us somewhere in between the two extremes, the changes can be maddening. God mode solves those problems.

Simply create a new folder on the desktop and name it this:

GodMode.{ED7BA470-8E54-465E-825C-99712043E01C}

When you open the folder, you will find access to every setting possible without getting into direct manipulation of the code. For those who do like to tweak their computers at least a little bit, this will be a huge time saver as you no longer need to hunt through numerous programs and menus to find what you are looking for.

Touch Screen Gestures

I know, not everyone has a touch screen so this is not universally relevant, but it is prevalent enough that it warrants its own section.

Pinch zoom – Move two or more fingers closer together or farther apart in order to zoom in and out, just as you do with most touchscreen devices.

Scrolling – Just swipe a finger up or down and you can scroll through any document with ease.

Task view – In addition to the icon, you can also activate Task view by swiping in from the left of the screen.

Action Center – The Action Center is activated by a swipe in from the right.

Closing an app – Swiping from top to bottom will automatically close any app.

Chapter 3 – Privacy Settings

In this strange age in which we live, it seems as though everyone is always watching, whether we want them to or not. To that end, Windows 10 makes it possible to greatly increase your privacy above the default settings.

Do not track – This is an Edge feature that will come already turned on. The purpose is to prevent websites from gathering information about your browsing and search habits as well as location.

Start menu – If you don't want nosy people knowing what apps you have recently installed or use the most often, you can turn off those features in the Personalization settings.

Location – Speaking of location, all kinds of apps these days want to know where you are. You can actually deny them access by going to Settings > Privacy >

Location where you can turn off the feature for every app with one click. If want to customize things more, you can leave the Location toggle on and simply turn it off for all the apps you don't want tracking your location.

Camera – You would be surprised by how many apps want to use your camera. I for one have no idea why CNN thinks it needs to use mine. Or my printer app. Such things truly boggle the mind. In any case, the Privacy settings let you turn off each app's access to your camera so you can be reasonably certain that Wolf Blitzer isn't spying on you.

Getting to know you – Microsoft likes to collect data on the people who use their products, like most companies these days. Sometimes it is for marketing, sometimes (as in this case) it is to learn how you speak and write so that they can develop better voice and hand recognition software. Fortunately, you don't have to let them.

Simply click the Stop getting to know me button and it will stop. Cortana will also forget everything she already knows about you.

These are just a handful of things you can control. You can also deny access to your contacts, account info, calendar, email, messaging, Bluetooth radios and more.

Another privacy setting not actually in the privacy settings is to turn off Peer-to-Peer updates. This is basically a feature that allows one computer to send update files to other computers on the network. To be fair, I'm not sure this is really a privacy issue, but if you want to test an update on one computer for a while before updating the rest of the computers on your network, then this is probably a good thing to turn off.

You do need to dig deep for this one though. Settings > Update & Security > Windows Update > Advances Options > Choose how updates are delivered will get you there. Finally, turn it off and you are set.

Hidden in Plain Sight

Have some information you want hidden from the general public? You can actually create a folder on your desktop without a name or icon.

Here is the rundown:

- Create a folder

- Right click and go to properties

- Select change icon

- Select a blank icon and hit OK and Apply

- The folder has now disappeared

- Right click on the folder again

- Select Rename

- Hold the Alt key, and using the number pad, press 0160

- Hit Enter

- The name is now gone and you have a completely hidden folder

If you lose it, you can just hit Ctrl + A and it will select al icons, including the hidden ones.

Chapter 4 – What's Netxt?

You might have heard while you were browsing about on a news site that Windows 10 is actually the last version of the operating system from the fine folks a Redmond. How can this be you ask? Is Windows dead? Are they going to have another OS with a different name?

Worry not citizen of the internet. Microsoft is simply moving away from the traditional model of software development in which a whole giant piece of software is developed and then released to the public for $120.

Instead, they are simply going to continually release new updates for the software, with new fixes and features as often as necessary. Clearly, Microsoft believes that their source code is flexible enough to allow them to tweak and stretch it for the foreseeable future. Others, such as Adobe have gone a similar route, eschewing regular releases of a physical product in favor of continuously updated software all connected in the cloud.

No doubt, at some point in the future a new interface technology or change in chip architecture will force Microsoft and everyone else to go back to the drawing board and release a brand new operating system built from the ground up. But those developments seem to be fairly far in the future.

In the meantime, Microsoft's first significant update based on this new model is set to be released in just a few days from the time I am writing this. In fact, it should already be available for download by the time you are able to read it.

The first thing to note is that the Anniversary Update was developed with extensive input from users. Microsoft started an Insider program that allows members (it's free for those who are interested) to test out new features months before they are released. And not just a few users.

There are nearly 10 million members of the insider program as of this writing. That means this new update was developed with input from a population the size of New York City using it for months with the ability to provide suggestions on what to keep, what to dump and what to create, rather than the typical bug reporting that most beta testers are used to. This is the first time this has happened for a major operating system.

So, what is coming in the Anniversary Update? Here a handful of updates that you can look forward to in the very near future.

Chase-able Tiles – Remember those nifty little Live Tiles we talked about a few pages ago? They are getting an upgrade. If you recall, Live Tiles display the latest news and updates relevant to the app. Well, until the update, if you saw a tile you were interested and clicked on it, it would only open the app.

So now you have to hunt for the information that interested you in the first place. Personally, I have found this pretty annoying. But no more! Chase-able Tiles will take you directly to the information that prompted your clicking to begin with. No longer will you have to hunt to find the latest sports scores.

Action Center – Some have found the Action Center to be lacking a bit in functionality. Now, though, with changes to both the notifications and Quick Actions, those people should be much more satisfied.

Notifications can now be heavily customized, adjusting the size, adding images and more to certain notifications (dependent on app support). You can also do things like choose which apps have priority over others.

Let's face it, lots of apps are more important than others, though you still like to be notified when the sushi place downtown has a lunch special. Now, you can make sure the more important things show up at the top and are always visible without missing out on Dragon Rolls.

Your notifications can now be synched across multiple devices as well, including your Windows or Android phone thanks to a little help from Cortana. Not only are the notifications showing up everywhere you want them to, you can also dismiss them from all of your integrated devices at the same time.

The Quick Actions will now be fully customizable as well, rather than being completely set in stone like they had been.

Dark Mode – There has been an option to essentially change your theme to black since the release of Windows 10. However, Microsoft has now made this much more comprehensive, making it possible to set the default color for all of your apps to black with just a few clicks of the mouse or pokes of the screen. The advantage is that your display will use less battery without all the color.

Edge – There is a lot going on with this one, but the biggest is definitely the ability to add extensions. I know, Chrome and Firefox have always been able to do this. Why Microsoft is just now catching up, I don't know. But it is here now, so get ready to add in your pop-up and ad blockers.

Cortana – There is no way that Microsoft can do an update without upgrading its digital assistant. One of the big upgrades here is that you can ask Cortana to check the weather, play your favorite album and more from the lock screen. If that is sounding a bit like Amazon's Echo, you are on the right track.

Conclusion

One could easily fill up a few more pages with all of the features and customizable settings in Windows 10, both those currently available and those still to come. At the end of the day, Windows has managed to bounce back from the debacle that was Windows 8 and looks to be set to help regain some of Microsoft's lost glory.

If you have not upgraded by the time you have read this, you have unfortunately missed the opportunity to get Windows 10 for free. However, if you have a newer PC or Surface Pro that is running Windows 7 or 8, it would be worth it to upgrade and get in on what is probably Microsoft's best OS to date.

You can find it for under a hundred dollars and I would consider it money well spent if you use your computers for anything more than general emailing and entertainment.

With a little luck and determination, Microsoft will continue to build off of the success of Windows 10 and so help millions of users the world over get their work done faster, with a good deal less frustration. I for one have definitely benefited from many of the features outlined above and I'm sure you will as well.